DISCO FEVER

70's Coloring Book

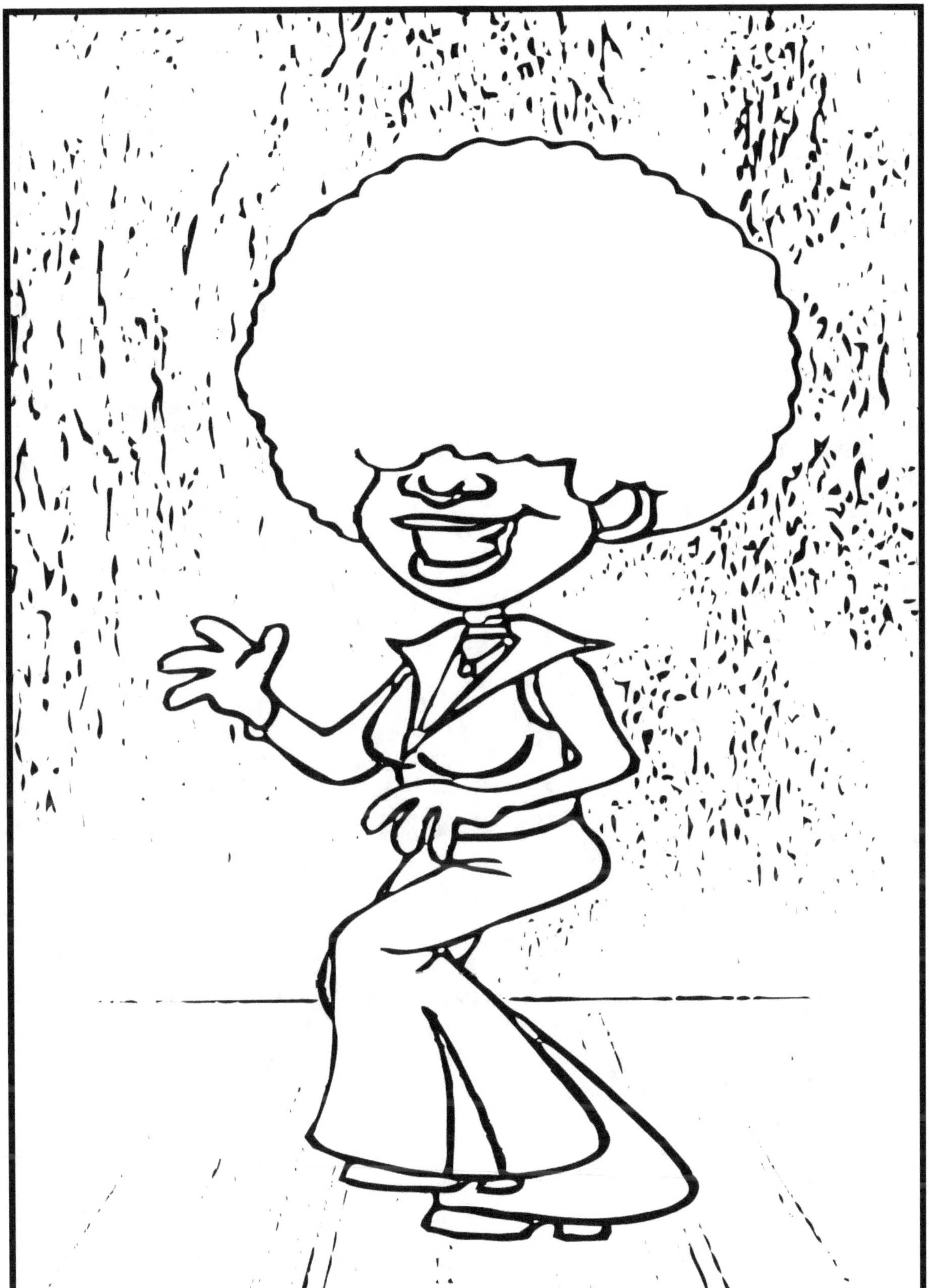

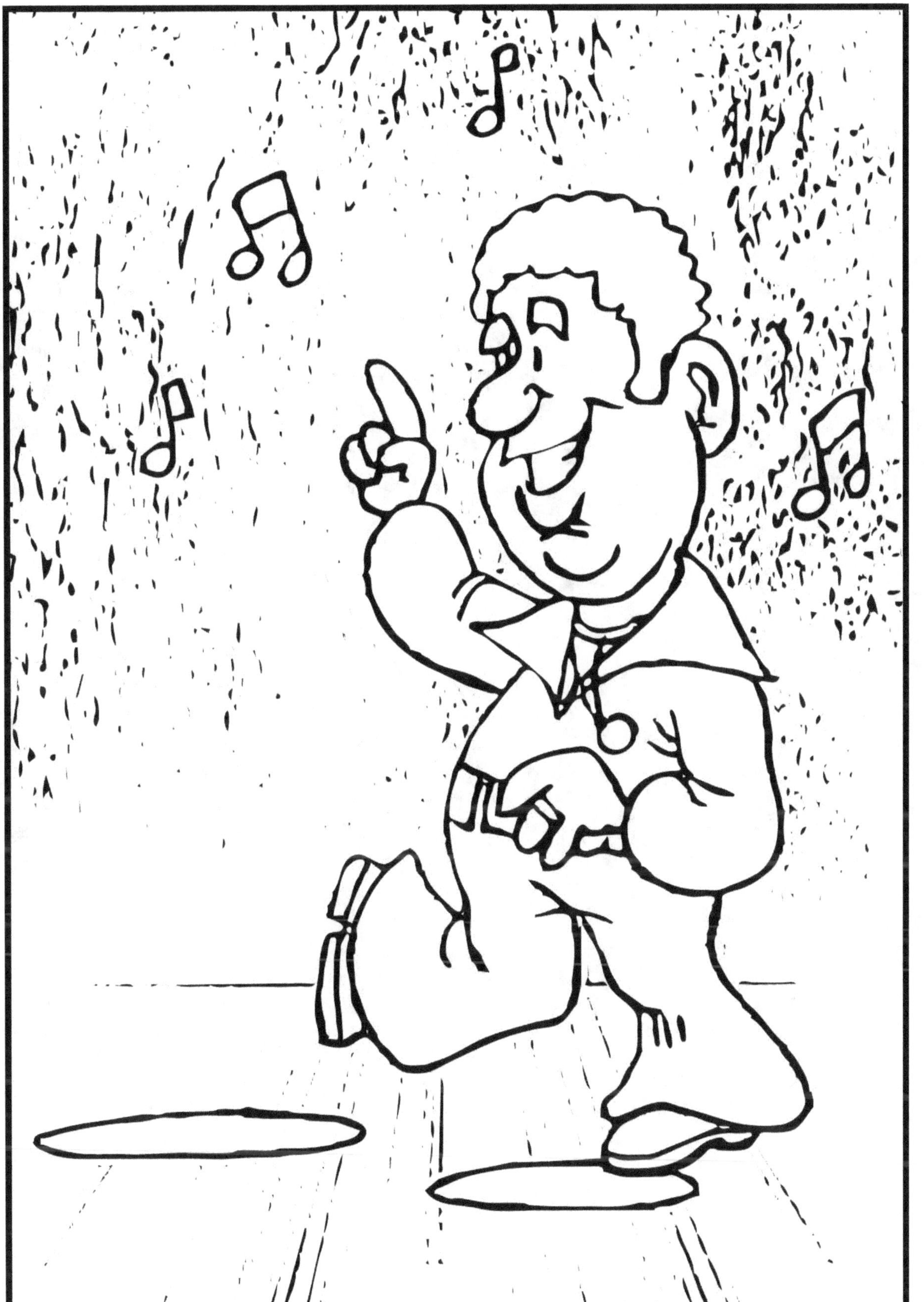

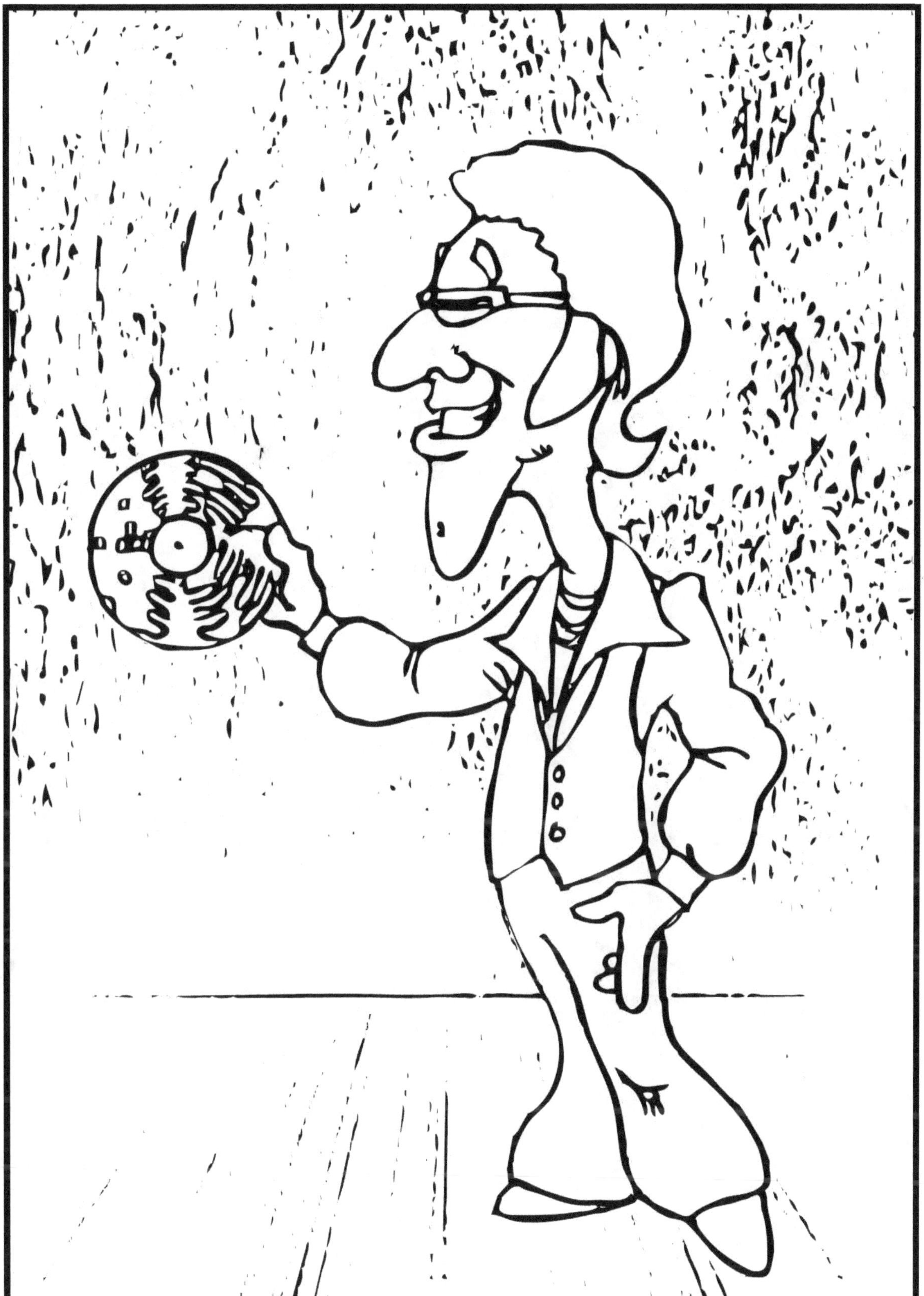

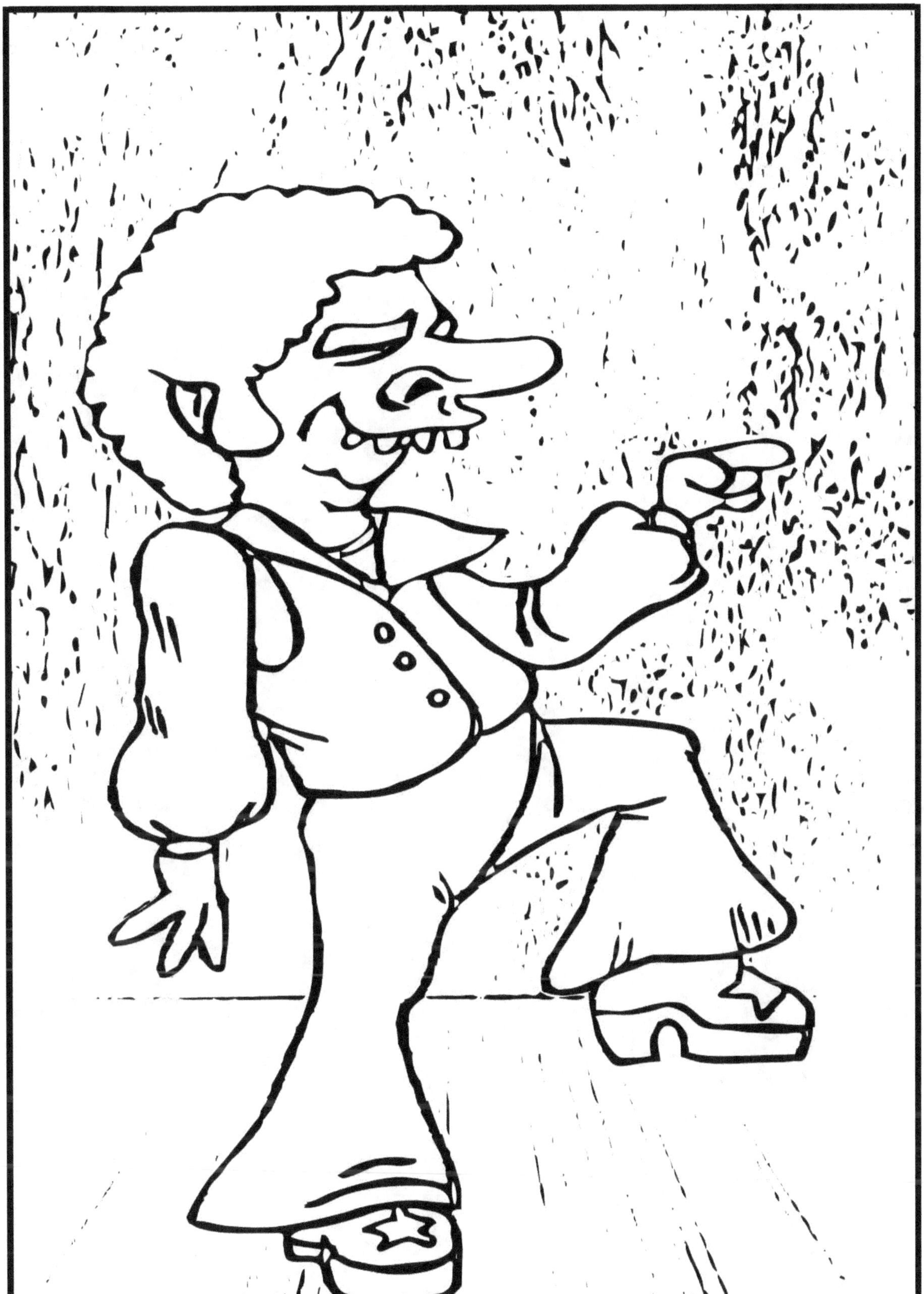

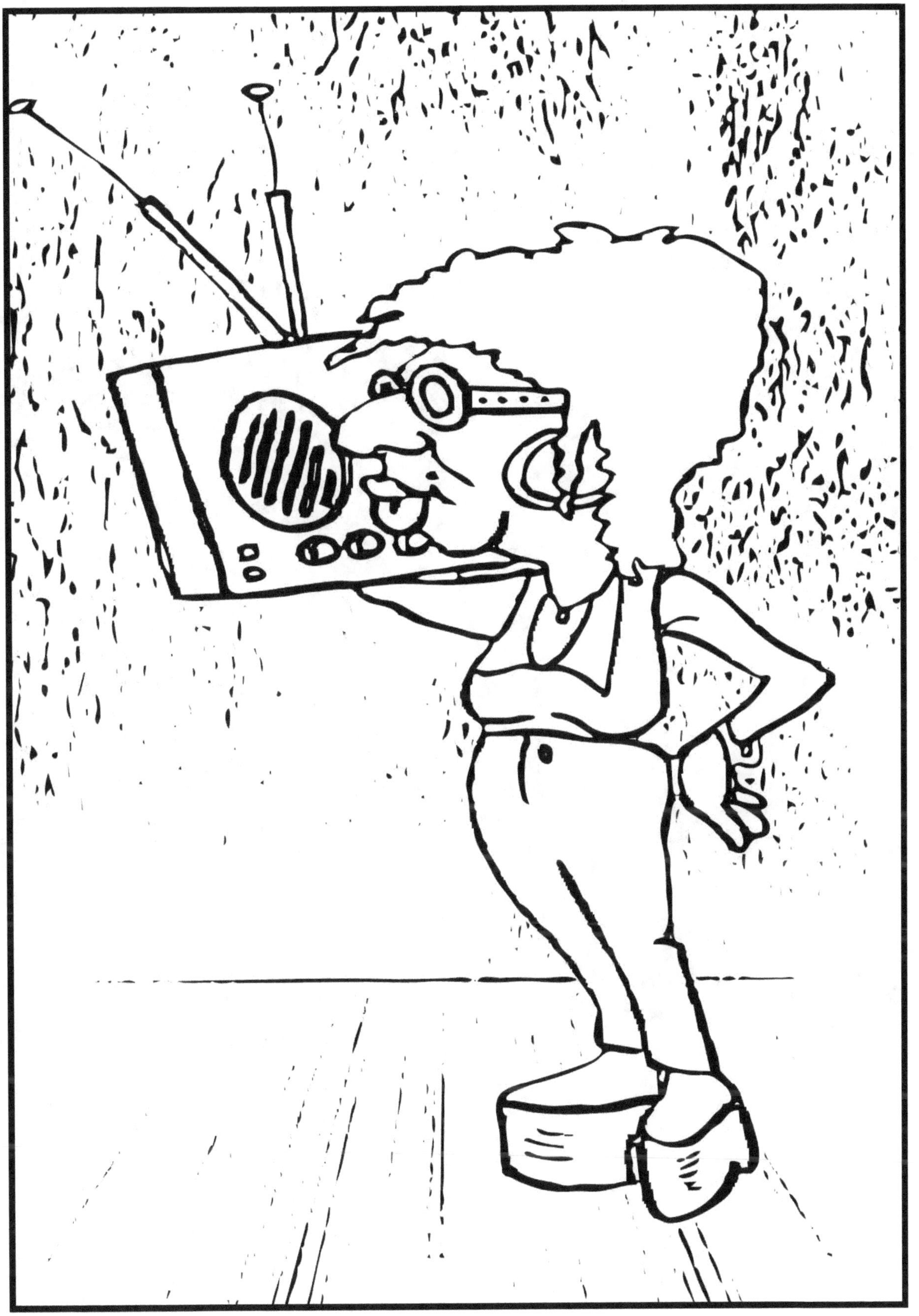

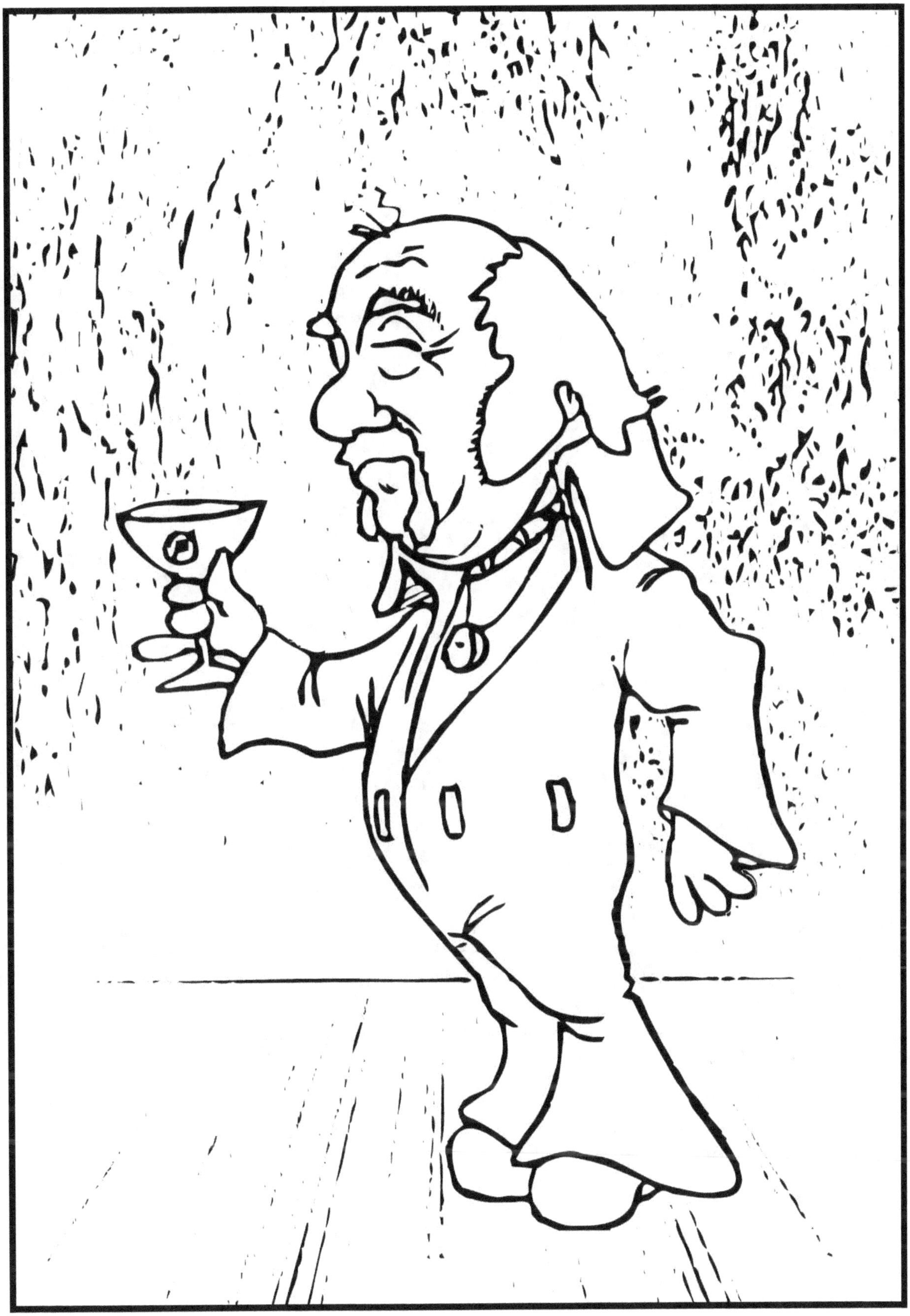

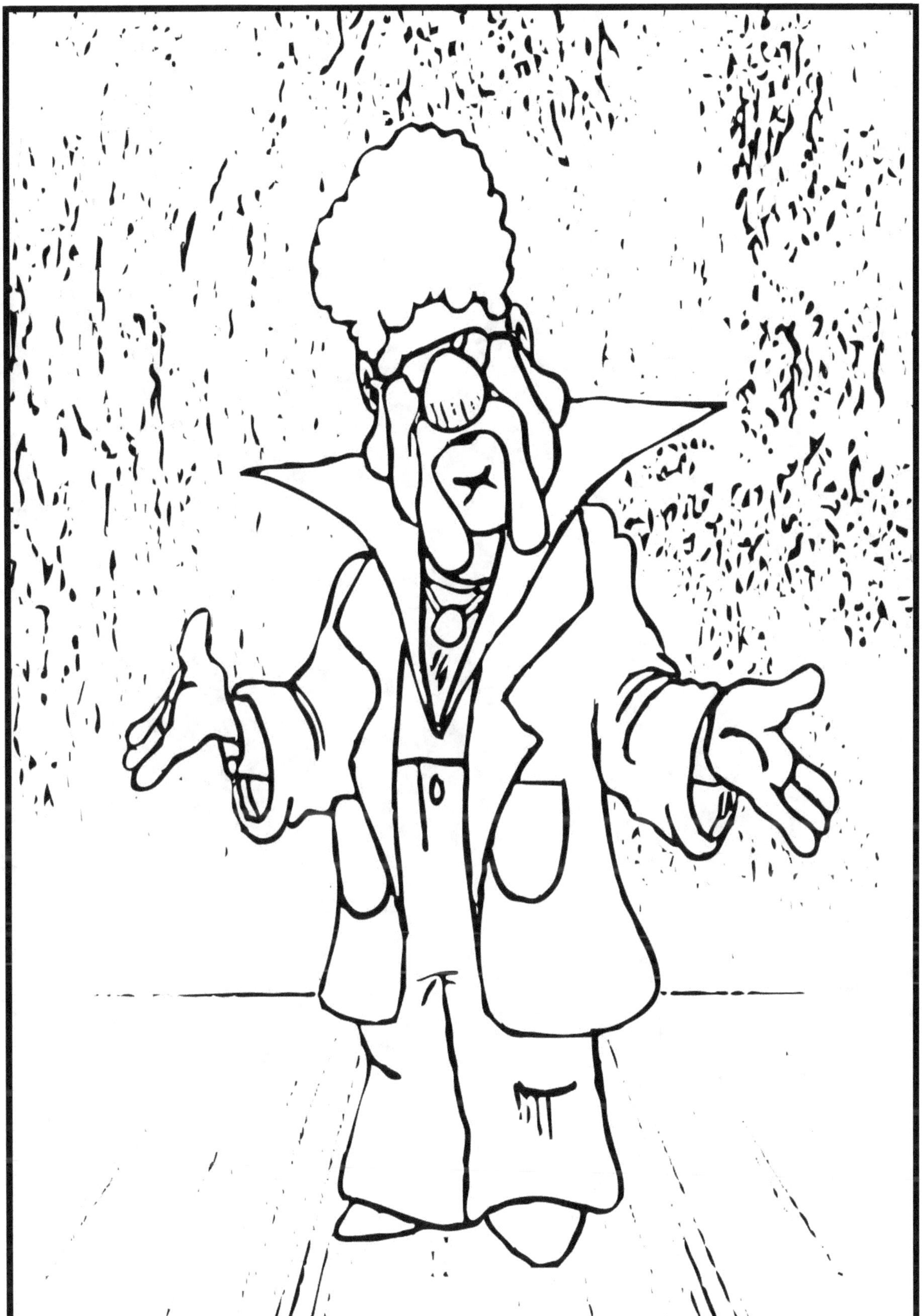

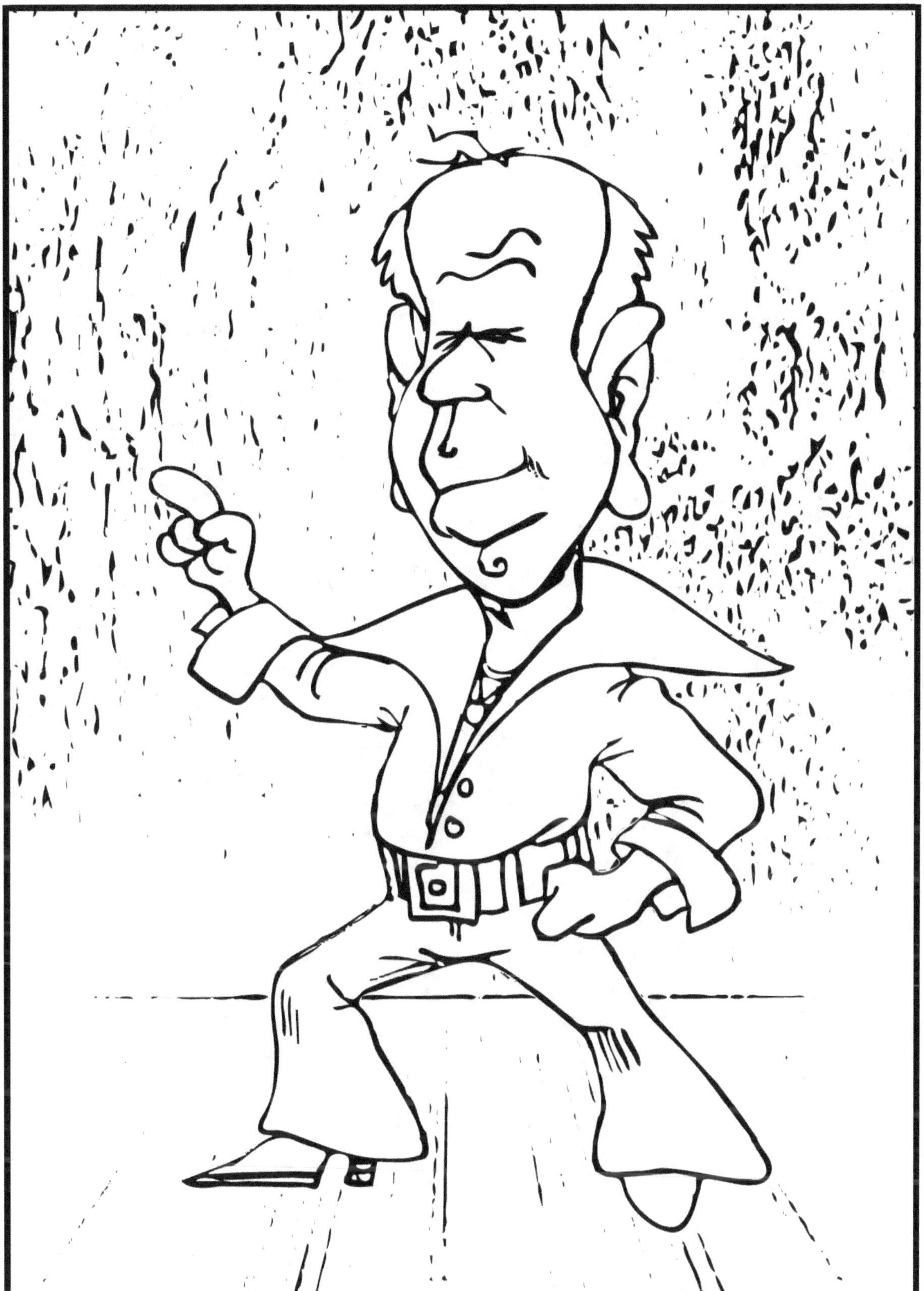

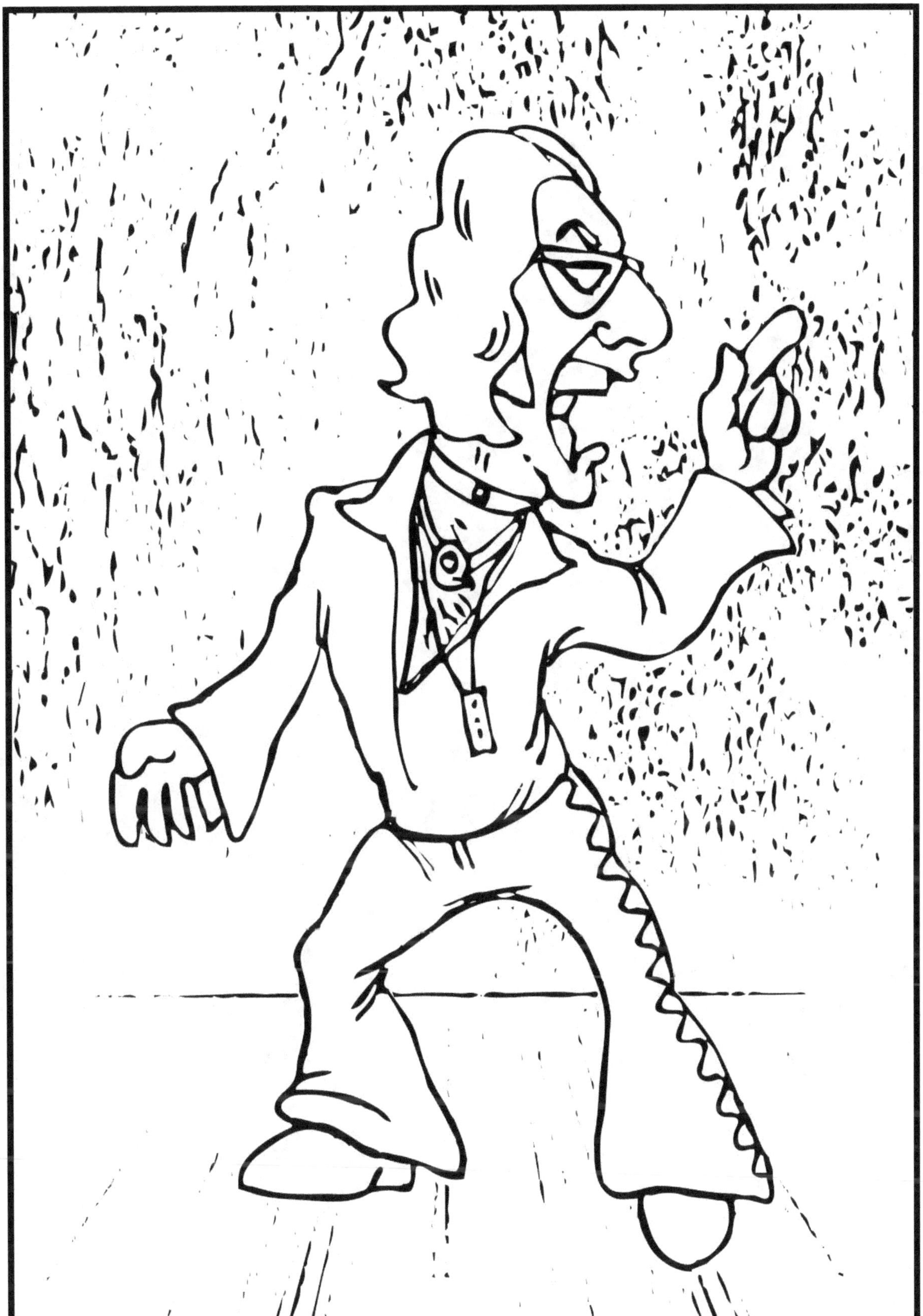

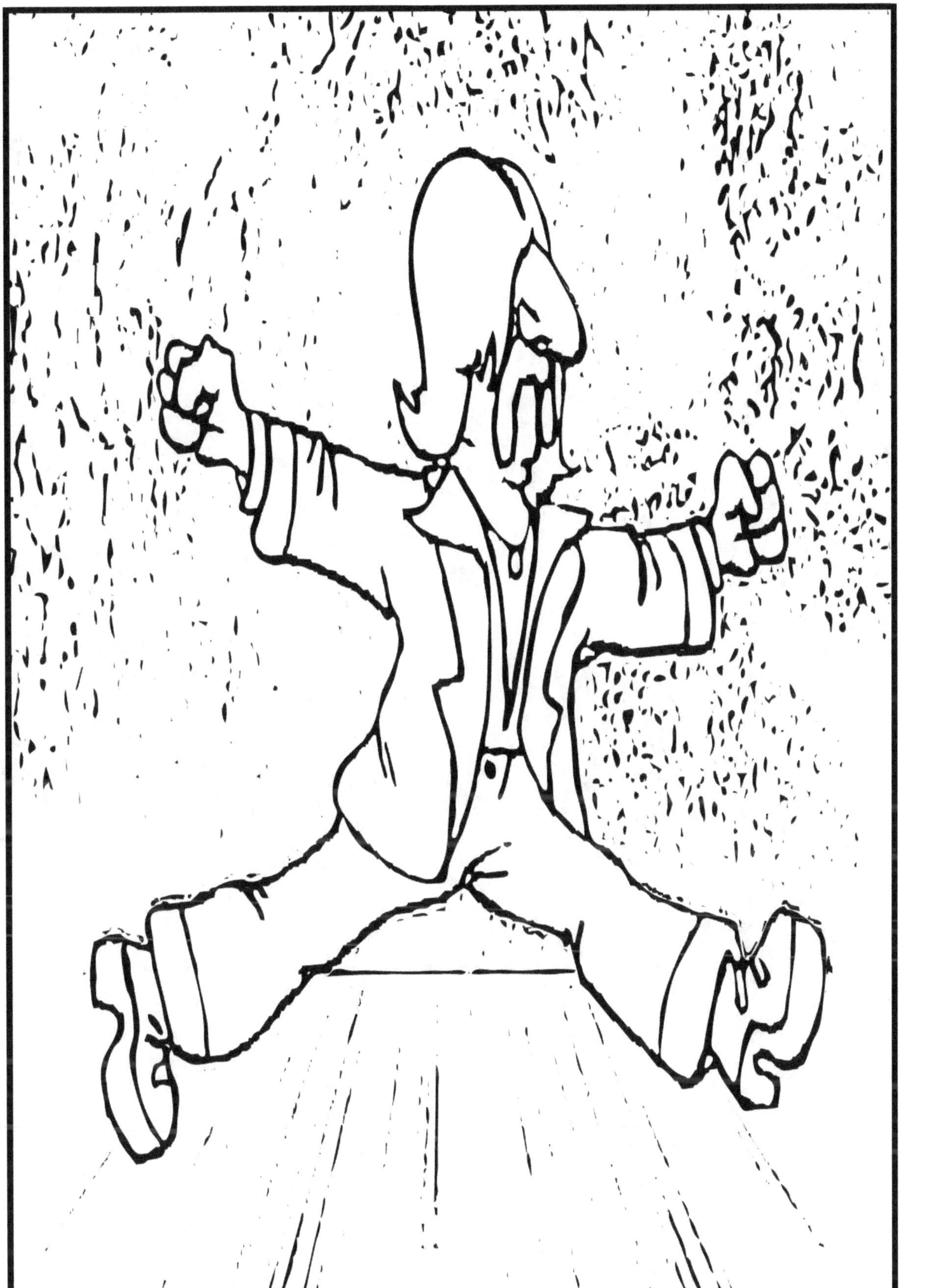

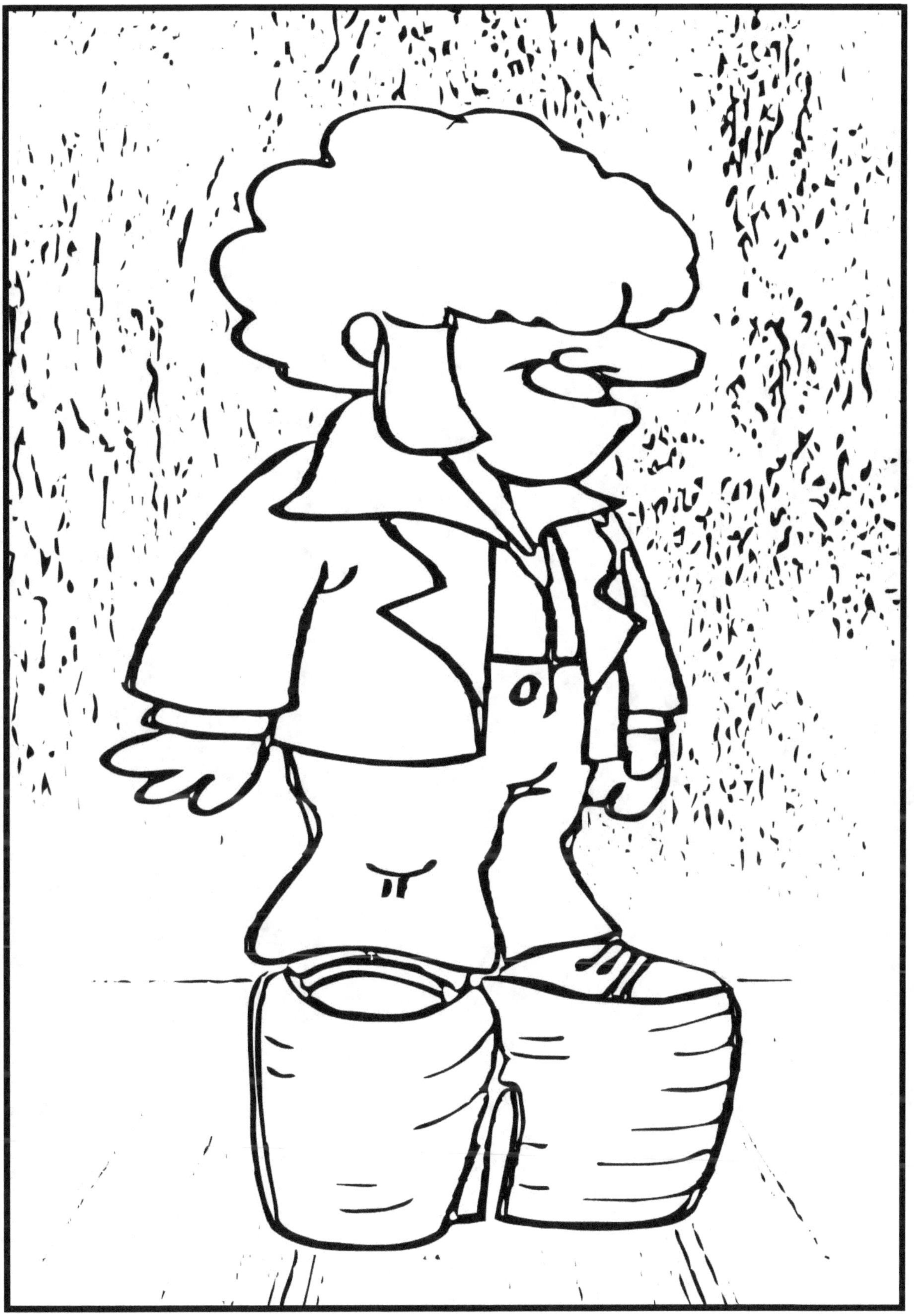

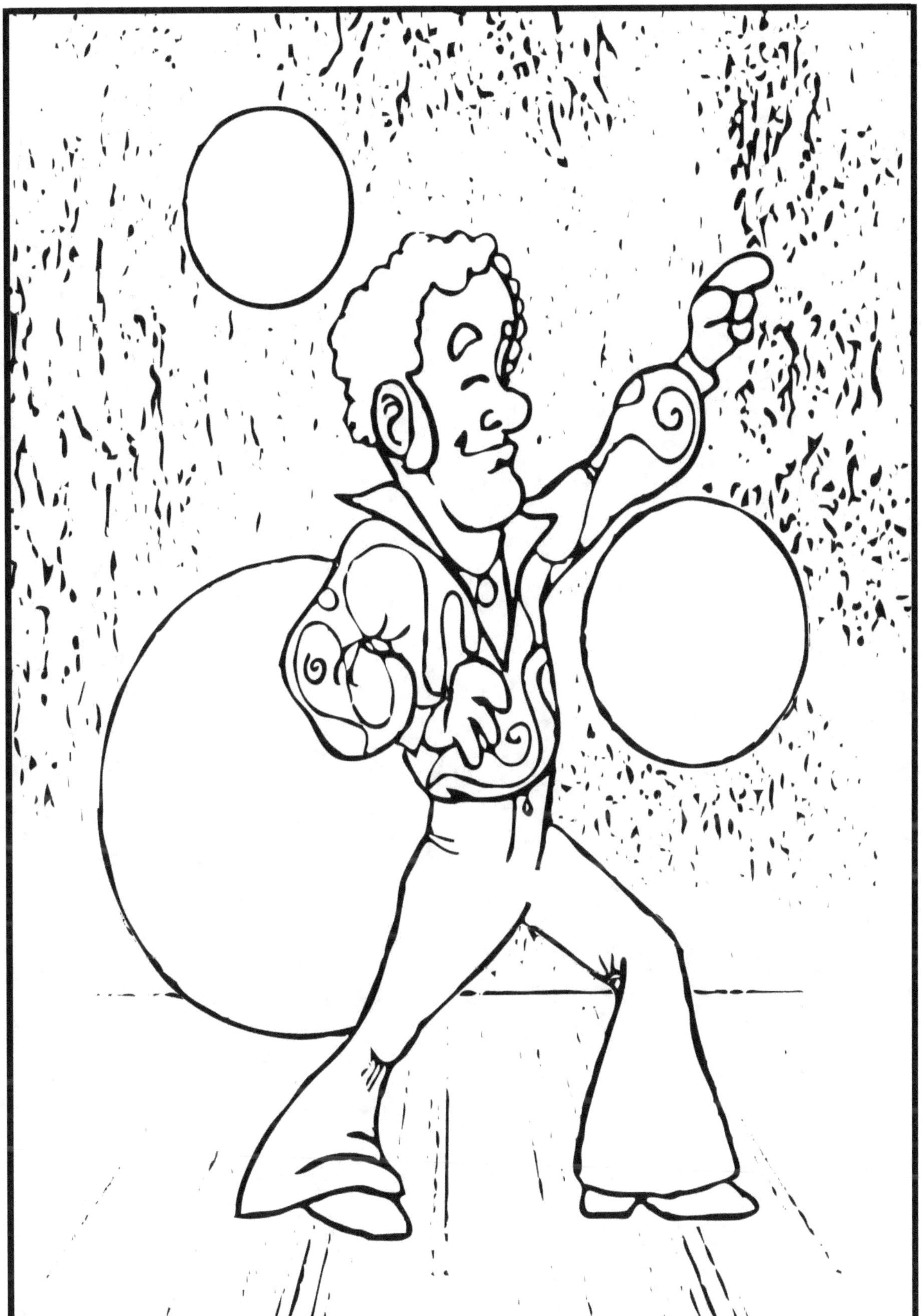

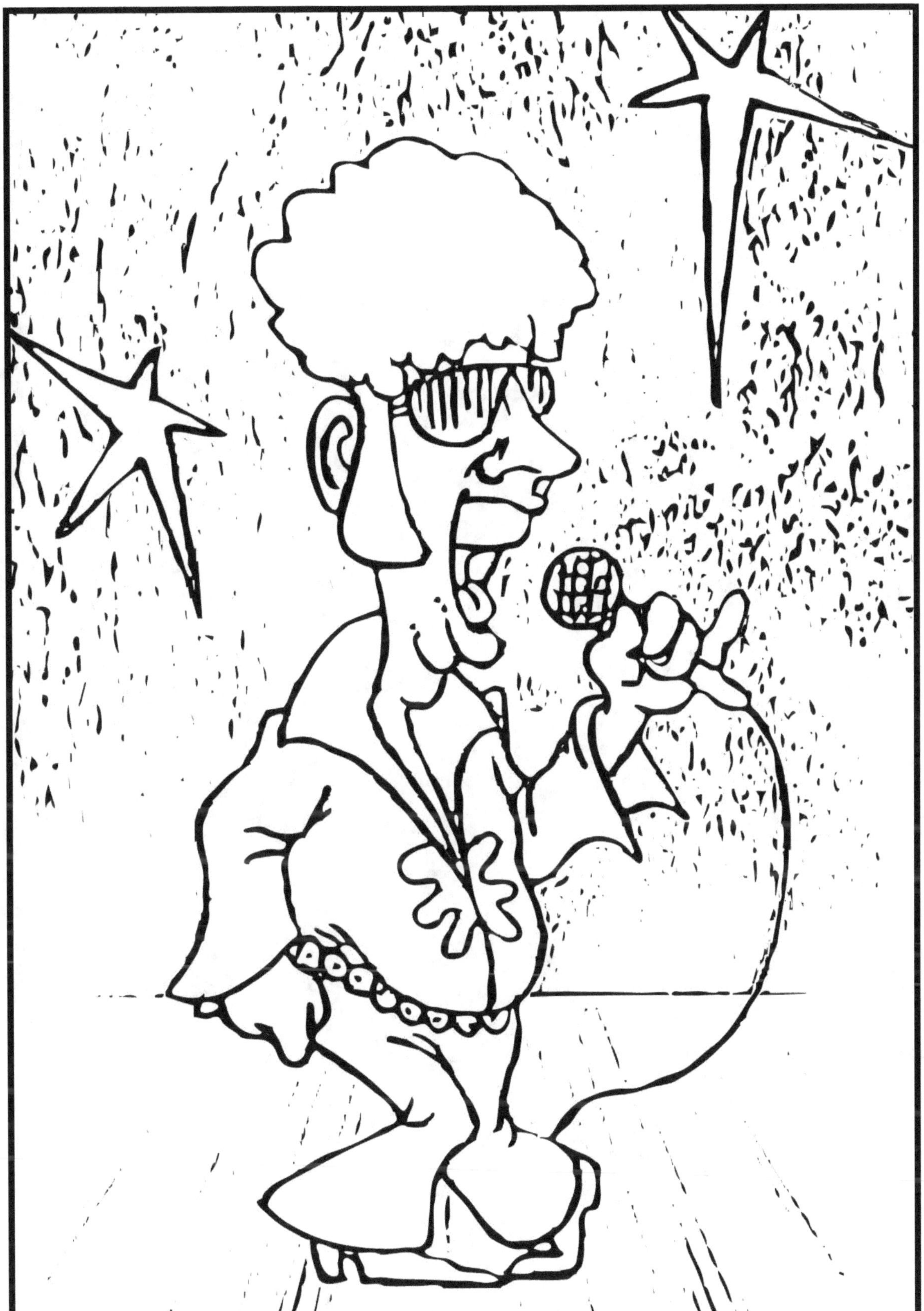

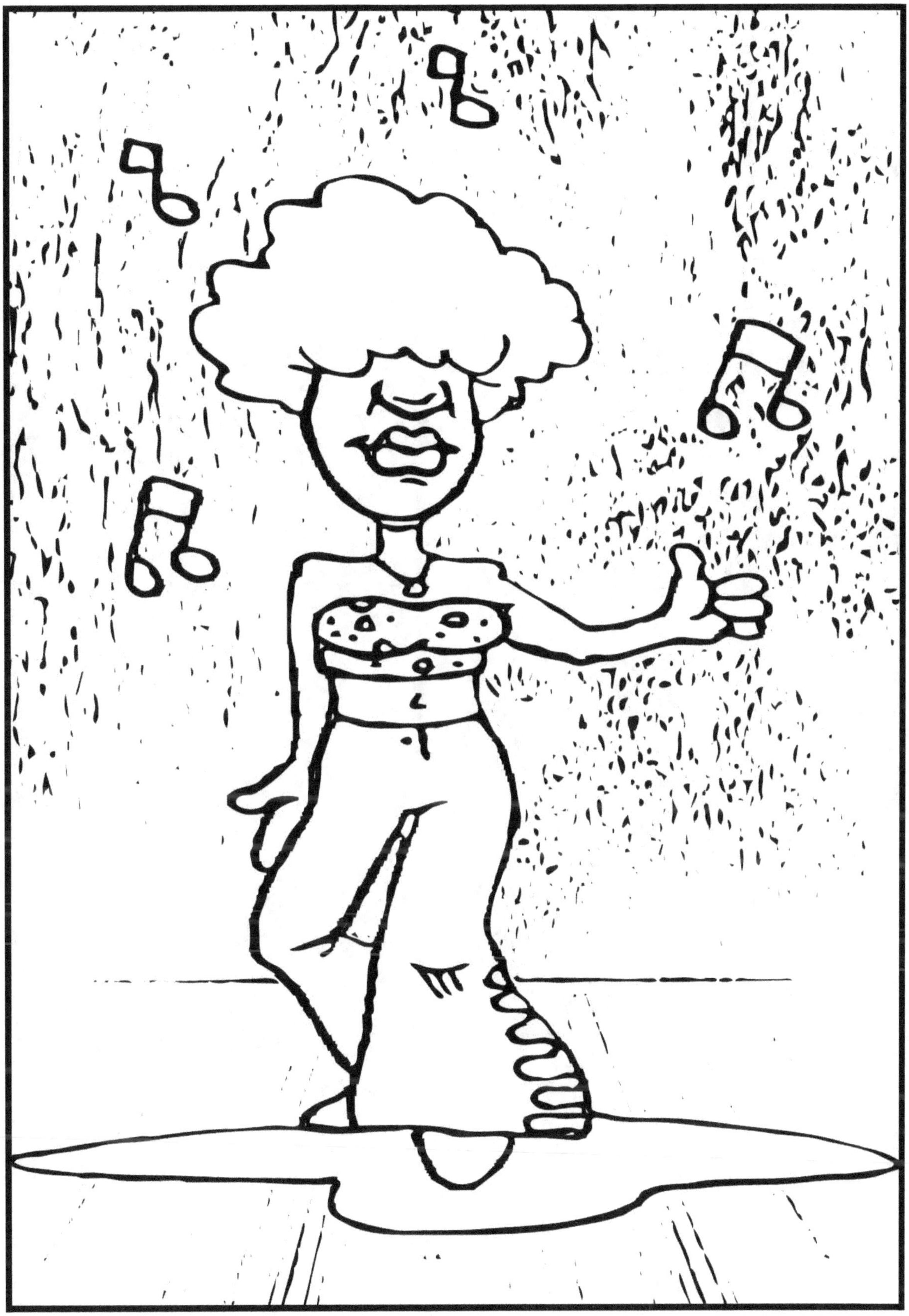

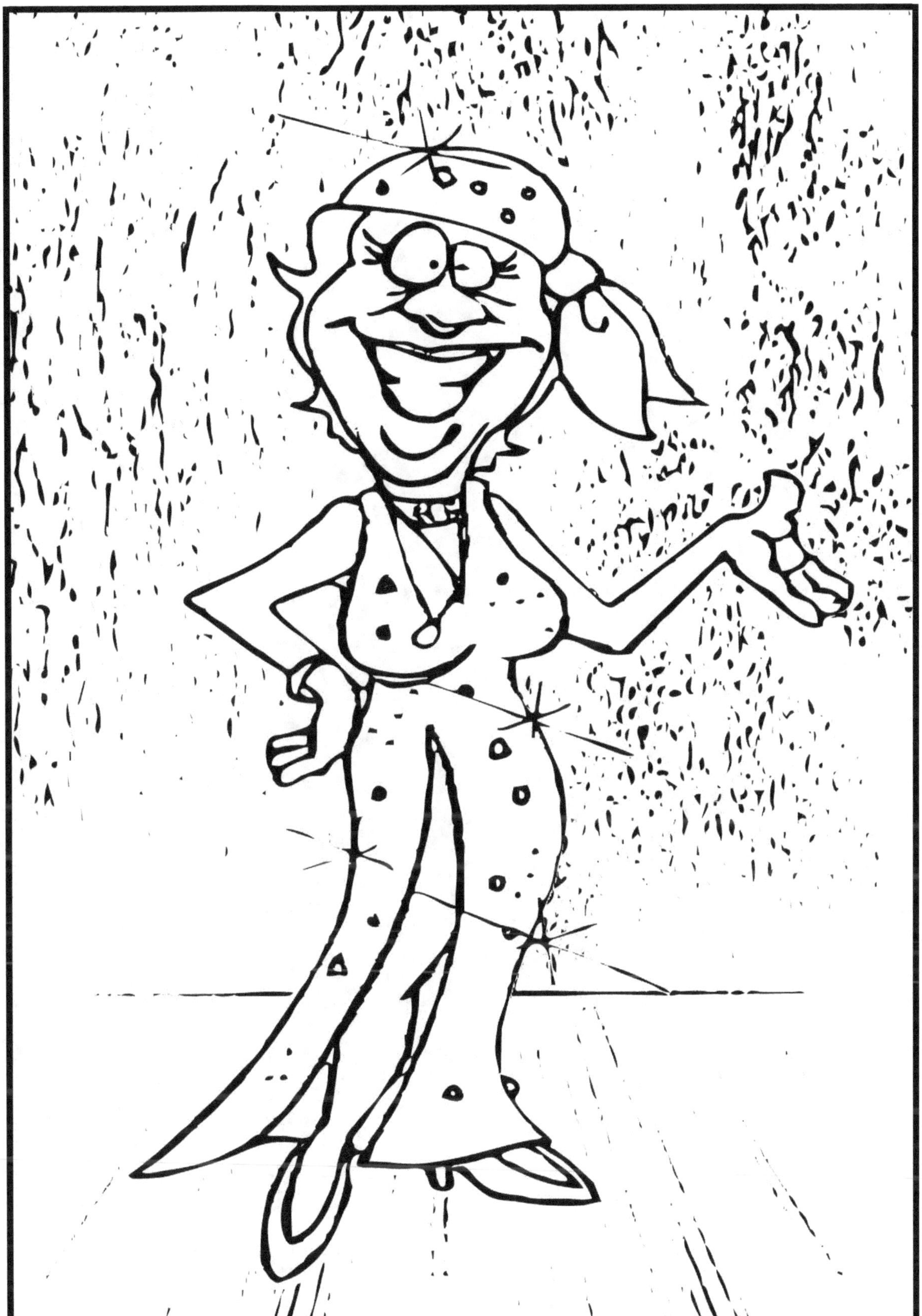

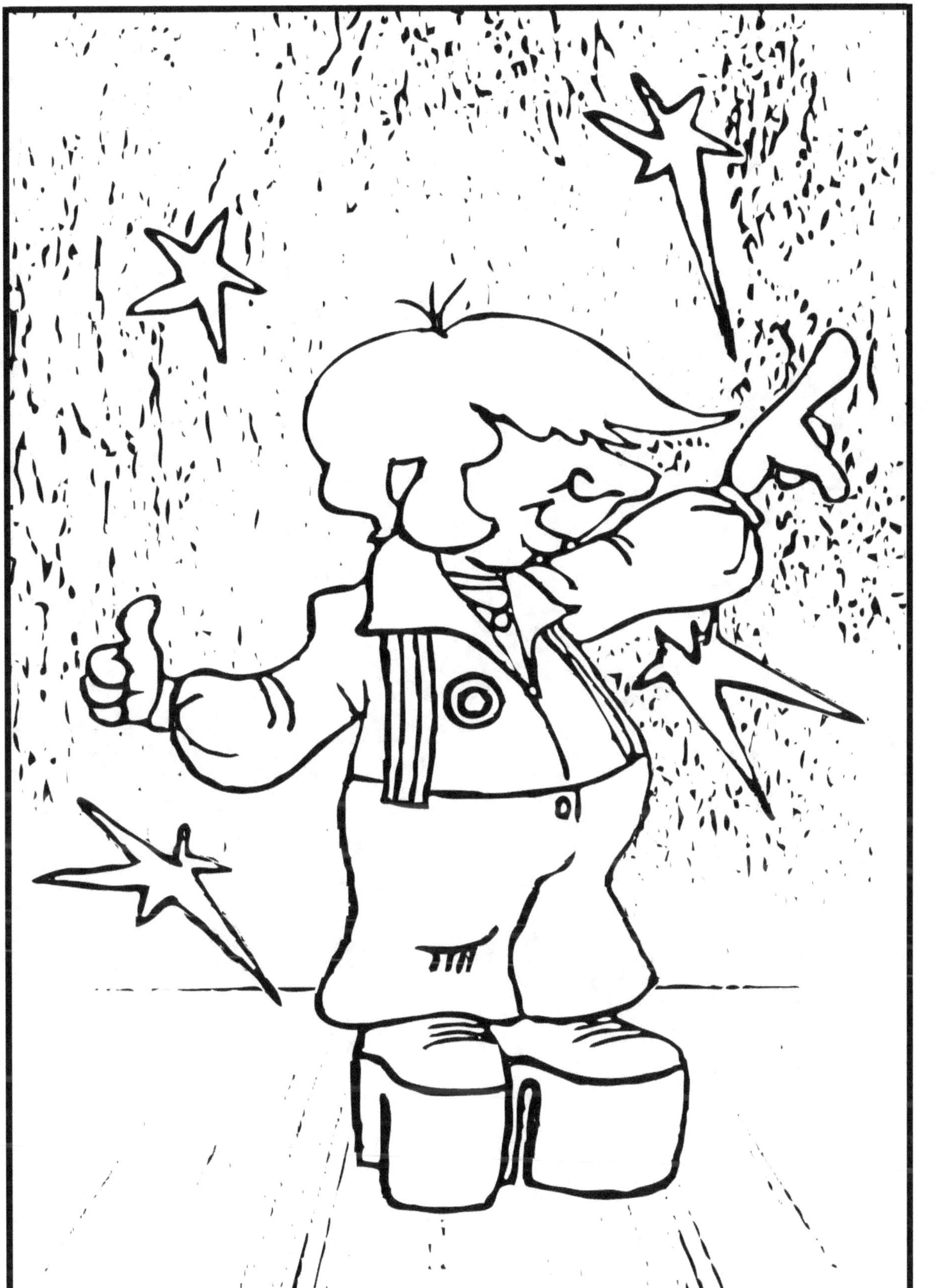

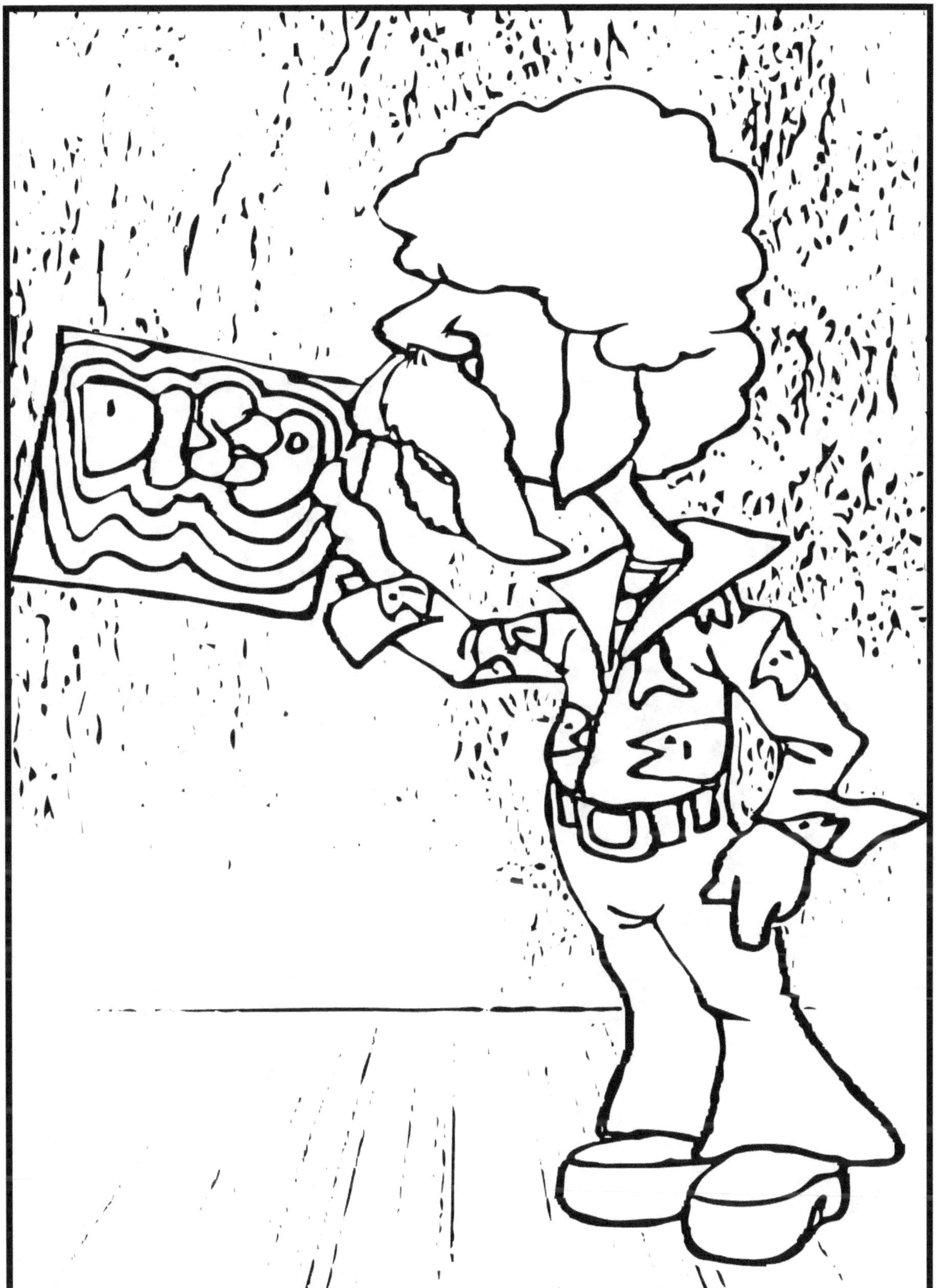
DISCO

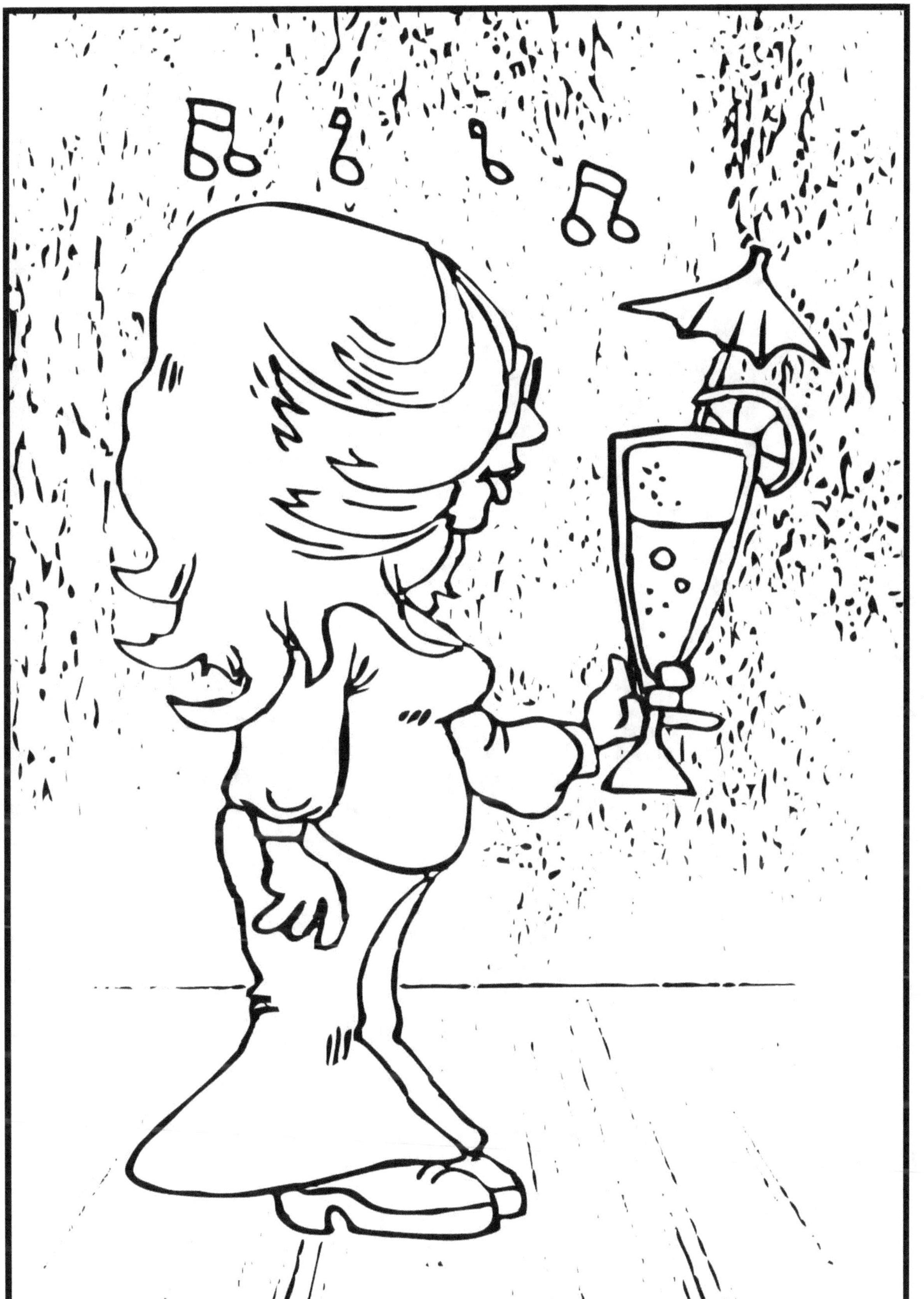

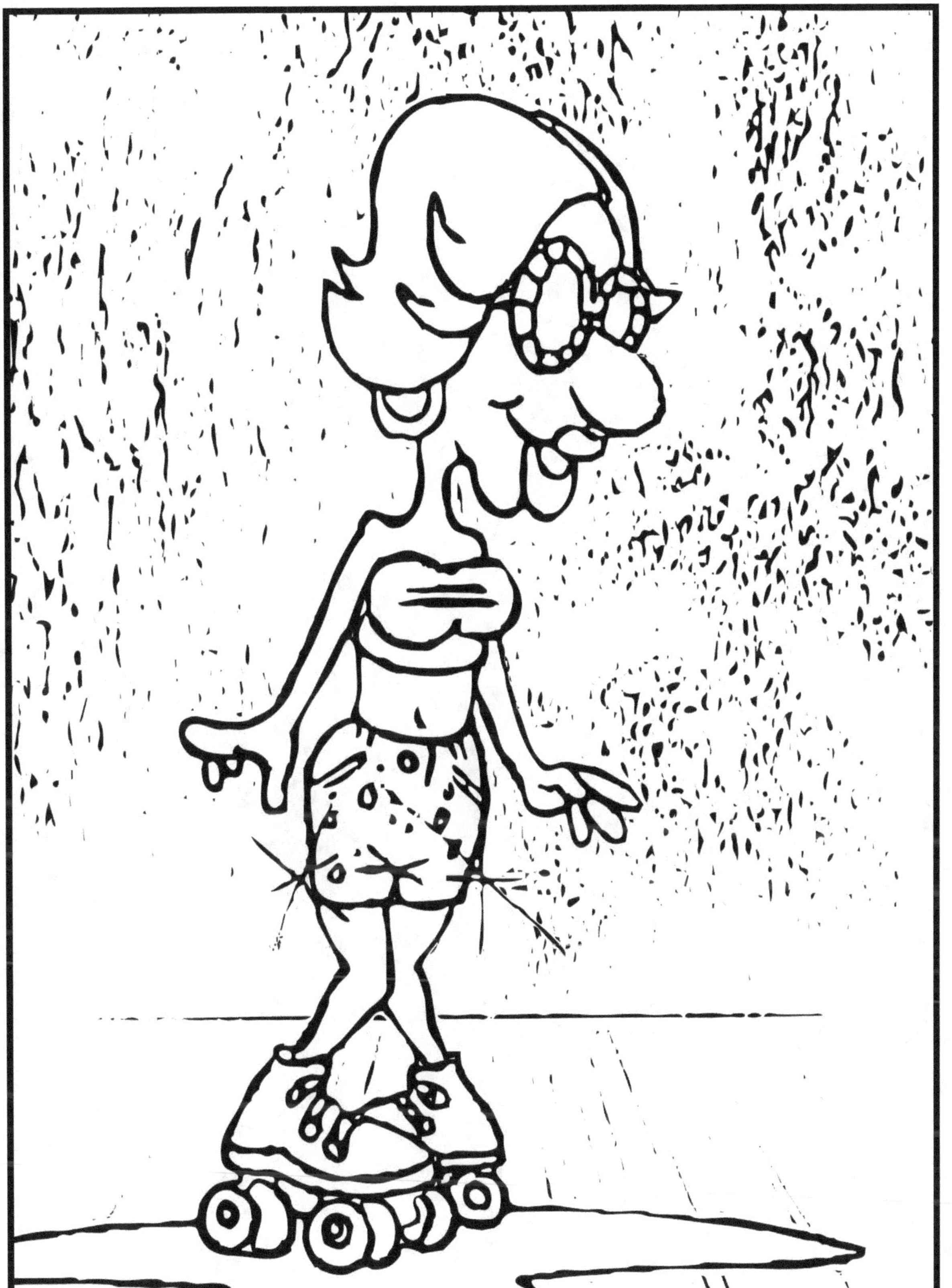

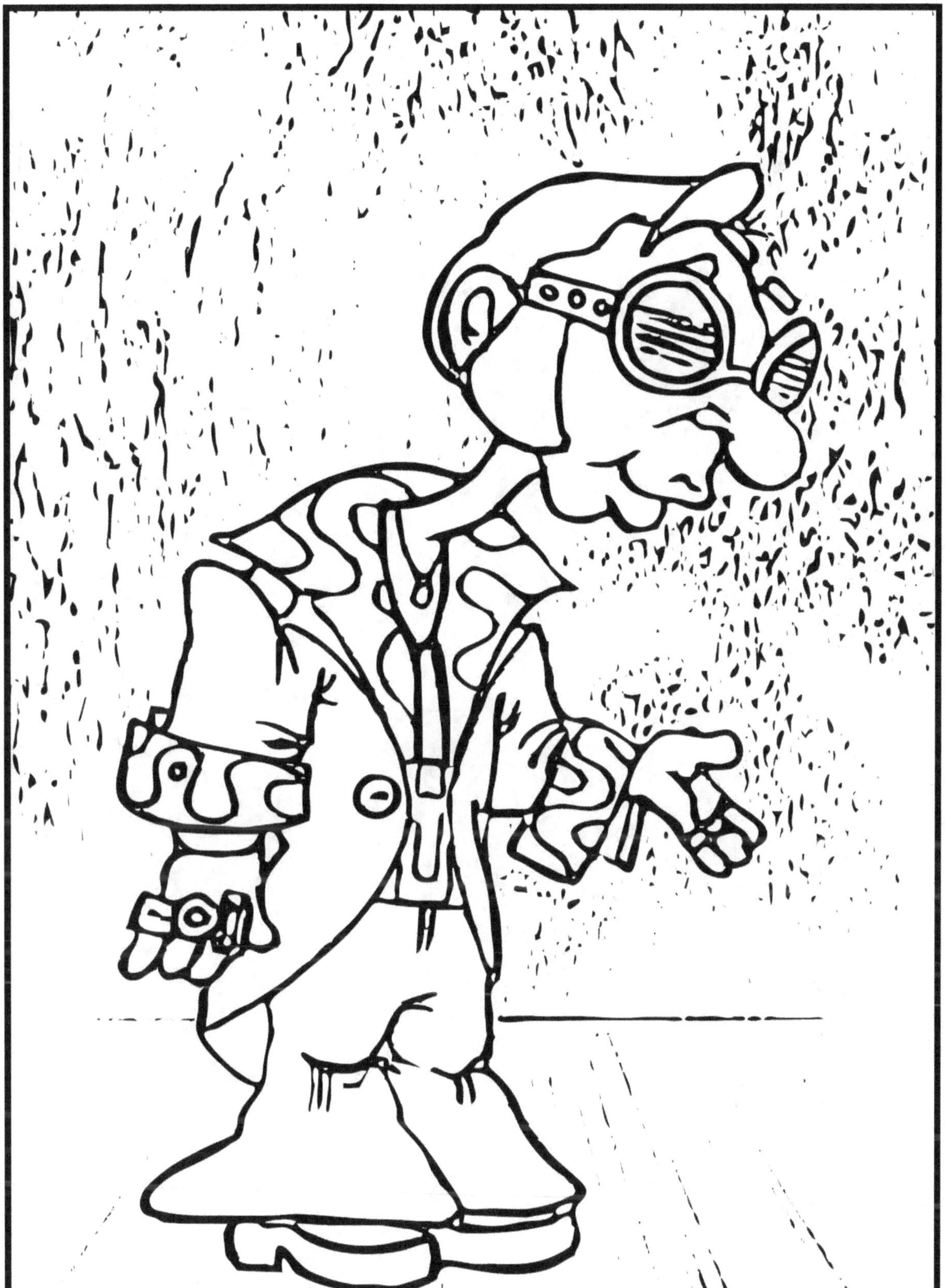

www.ingramcontent.com/pod-product-compliance
Lightning Source LLC
Chambersburg PA
CBHW081401170526
45166CB00010B/3165